DEVON LIBRARIE

GH01080152

Please return/renew this item by

Renew on tel. 0345 155 1001 or at

www.devon.gov.uk/libraries

SA

# Charlotte's
# kitchen

# RECIPES FROM

# Charlotte's kitchen

## Charlotte Lampard

Food and still life photography: Mark Davison

# Introduction

I am always delighted to take undeserved credit and so if Charlotte says that I suggested she write this book, how can I refuse to write the Introduction? My first wife, Marika Hanbury-Tenison, wrote innumerable cookery books and tested all the recipes on me, and so I suppose that sort of qualifies me. Marika was cookery editor of the Sunday Telegraph for 14 years and never missed a week's copy until she died in 1982. I know how much hard work goes into making recipes look easy and tempting. Charlotte has just the right light touch.

Marika, who pioneered this approach in the early '70s, would have approved of the way Charlotte does not blind the reader with exact amounts but allows the cook to use his or her imagination to make the dish fun and flexible. I have seen her do it on the many occasions when she came and gave cookery classes with Louella here on Bodmin Moor. Whenever I came into the kitchen there was an atmosphere of excitement, enthusiasm and surprise as the punters were taught new dishes and learned how easy it is to produce delicious food. Cooking should be fun and with Charlotte it is.

*Robin Hanbury-Tenison*

# Charlotte's kitchen

Cooking at The Kitchen gives me enormous pleasure. I have always had a need to feed people and this opportunity was heaven sent. Since coming back to Devon 18 years ago I have been doing cooking classes, specialising in recipes that take less than 20 minutes, and I have given these in Devon, Cornwall, Hampshire, Oxfordshire and London, but as I got older, and my children left home, having a small business with food seemed the next natural stage for me.

I have had wonderful staff to help me (as well as Rose Chanin above left) and everyday seems to bring a "story". We have romantic couples, families on their way to Cornwall and then coming back all brown and relaxed, regular people with their idiosyncrasies, and occasionally difficult customers, all in all a mixed bag. But I can honestly say there is not a day that I haven't enjoyed.

Now for some practicalities: You will see that I haven't listed salt and pepper in my recipes as I know that you are perfectly capable of realising that they are needed and you will also know how much or how little you like.

I have also not given the amounts these recipes will feed as that also depends on you and your family. A soup for a dinner party might feed eight but for a lunch probably only four. So these recipes fall between making enough for four to six.
*Charlotte Lampard*

# The Recipes

# Soups

# Butternut squash, lime and ginger soup

*3 tblsps olive oil*
*2 onions, chopped*
*5cm fresh ginger, chopped*
*Pinch of dried chilli*
*1 clove of garlic, optional*
*1 butternut squash, peeled*
  *and chopped*
*Stock*
*Zest and juice of 1 or 2 limes*

Heat the oil in a large pan and sauté the onions for a few minutes, until they are translucent. Add the ginger, chilli and garlic and cook for a further couple of minutes. Add the squash and cook for about 10 minutes making sure that they don't stick by stirring them from time to time. Add enough stock to just cover with the lime zest. Simmer until the squash is soft. Liquidise and add the lime juice.

I suggest that when you use a recipe for soup that you ignore the quantity of stock needed. Add just enough liquid to cook the vegetables and then add more to make the soup the way you like it. A thin soup is very difficult to thicken, but it is very easy to thin down by adding more stock or milk/cream.

WINE SUGGESTION
Yearlstone Number 1

# Thai vichysoisse

4 leeks, sliced
2 medium-sized potatoes,
  peeled and chopped
Sunflower oil
1 tin of light coconut milk
Stock
1 tsp Green Thai curry paste,
  add more if necessary
Juice of 1 lime
Zest and juice of 1 lemon
Chives

I love leek and potato soup – to me it is all the things a soup should be – smooth creamy and comforting. Try this version as something a little bit different. Years and years ago, in the '6os, there was a restaurant in London in Chelsea called Nick's Diner, and I knew the chef there. He told me that whenever a recipe didn't taste quite right but you couldn't think what it needed to try a spritz of lemon juice. When I make chicken stock I often add a bit of lemon that has been hanging around the kitchen.

Cook the leeks and potatoes in the oil for 5 minutes. Add the coconut milk and enough stock to cover the vegetables. Add the Thai curry paste and simmer until the vegetables are soft. Blend until really smooth. Add the lime juice. Just before serving add the lemon zest and juice and serve sprinkled with chives. Don't be too rigid in quantities when making soup – a little bit more or less isn't going to make too much difference nor is using lemon juice instead of lime.

The main danger with soup, I think, is adding too many ingredients – keep it to two or three rather than emptying the leftovers into the pot. That can work sometimes but I don't really recommend it. It can look very dingy and taste confused.

WINE SUGGESTION
Yearlstone Number 1

# Pea and mint soup with feta cheese

*50g butter*
*1 onion, roughly chopped*
*350g potatoes, peeled and*
*chopped into cubes*
*Stock*
*1 bunch of fresh mint*
*500g frozen peas*
*200ml crème fraiche*
*100g of feta cheese, cubed*

This is what I call instant soup. I usually have feta in the fridge, even at home, and we must surely all have peas in the freezer. I always buy petits pois rather than the ordinary pea as they are just so much nicer. This soup is a very pretty pale green. If you come to the kitchen and this is on the menu you could probably guess that we have been very busy and I have had to make this as a standby.

Melt the butter in a pan and sweat the onion for 5 minutes. Add the potatoes and enough stock to cover the vegetables. Add 3 sprigs of mint and bring to the boil. Simmer for 10 minutes until the potatoes are cooked. Add the peas and cook for 3 minutes. Blend until smooth. Return the soup to the pan, stir in the crème fraiche. Heat gently. Season. Chop more mint and add to the soup just before serving with the feta crumbled on top.

Try not to re-heat this soup as the colour does go 'off' after a bit. Serve in white bowls if possible as the colour really does have an impact. I usually add a few whole peas as well.

WINE SUGGESTION
Yearlstone Number 2

# Starters

# Kedgeree

*There are plenty of recipes for this with all sorts of complicated additions but this is the one I prefer above all. Deliciously buttery with a little spice and lemon juice.*

*375g smoked haddock or cod,
   undyed*
*1 tsp turmeric*
*250g basmati rice*
*150g butter*
*2 tsps curry powder*
*Juice of 1 lemon*
*3 hard-boiled eggs, quartered*
*Parsley*
*Lemon wedges*

I served this at my eldest daughter's wedding; I spent the Friday cooking this for 120! I live in a very quiet valley and on the side of a hill so we had to go for a bucolic wedding. No marquees or seating plans just a glorious relaxed occasion. Kedgeree seemed to fit the bill perfectly as nearly everyone could eat it, unless they were vegans. A tomato salad is the only accompaniment needed. One plate and one fork – so easy to serve and everyone seemed to enjoy it. Canapés to begin with, kedgeree and then tiny meringues and bite-sized éclairs. Ideal for a simple meal – perfect for a Bridge supper – just cover the dish with foil and put it in the oven at 180c/gas 4 for about 25 minutes.

Cover the fish with water in a large pan and bring to the boil. Simmer for 1 minute and leave in the water for about 5 minutes.
Lift the fish from the water but keep the water. Let the fish cool and when it is cool enough, flake with your fingers, taking off the skin and removing any bones. Bring the fishy water back to the boil, add the turmeric and some salt and the rice.

Cook the rice for 10 minutes then drain. Meanwhile melt the butter with the curry powder and lemon juice and mix it into the rice well. Transfer to a serving dish and place the hard-boiled eggs on top. Sprinkle with parsley and serve with lemon wedges.
I add some prawns to the mixture just before serving if I want to lift it to another level.

WINE SUGGESTION
Yearlstone Number 1

# Smoked fish chowder

700g *smoked haddock,*
*undyed*
*Milk to cover*
*1 tblsp oil*
*25g butter*
*150g bacon lardons*
*4 medium salad potatoes,*
*diced*
*2 medium leeks, finely sliced*
*1 tsp turmeric*
*Fresh chopped parsley*

Real comfort food. Whenever I serve this at The Kitchen it sells out immediately. You could add a few prawns, as I do, to make it look a bit more special. Again as with the kedgeree I add some turmeric. Not only does this make the colour more appealing it also has health giving properties: helpful for cancer, arthritis and Alzheimer's. In the old days, we used haddock that had been artificially dyed with 'e' numbers – now we don't do that so we have to add the colour again.

I live on my own now and I love having friends to stay for the weekend and this is perfect for a Saturday lunch. Satisfying enough after walking, shopping, etc, in the morning and yet it won't spoil your appetite for the main event of the weekend – Saturday night dinner!

Put the haddock in a shallow pan and cover with the milk. Simmer for 5 minutes, drain off the milk into a bowl or jug. When the fish is cool enough, take off the skin and flake, removing bones. Heat the oil and butter in a pan and cook the bacon lardons until beginning to be crisp, add the potatoes, leeks and turmeric and cook for a few minutes. Add the reserved milk and cook covered in the pan until soft. Season and stir in the fish and the parsley.

WINE SUGGESTION
Yearlstone Number 1

*Pippy the cat. Yearlstone, 1995-2009*

# The Kitchen Plate

*This plate of appetizers is by far and away the most popular item on the menu and the one I enjoy preparing most.*

Nothing too heavy but lots of interesting flavours and textures. Sitting outside on the Terrace with a Kitchen Plate and a glass of wine is pretty much heaven for me.

It is a great excuse to create tasty things I don't have room for on the menu like the Tapenade and butter bean puré, griddled courgettes, anchovies, that old favourite egg mayonnaise, ratatouille, tortilla – I am sure you will be able to think of lots more things to add.

The salami and cured meats come from Cornwall and I can get these in the market in Tiverton. I have got some decorative plates which I use – they are all different – and the selection of things changes all the time.

It is good plate to share as a starter or a lightish lunch for one.

## TORTILLA/FRITTATA

I am never quite sure what the difference is except that one is Spanish and the other Italian. Perhaps someone can tell me? There are lots of variations on this theme. Sliced courgettes with Parmesan are very good.

*2 tblsps olive oil*
*1 onion, thinly sliced*
*5-6 cooked salad potatoes, sliced*
*5 eggs, beaten*
*Handful of grated cheese*

Heat the olive oil in a pan and cook the onion until soft and translucent. Add the potatoes and cook through. Beat the eggs in a large bowl and add the onions and potatoes to the eggs. Mix well. Heat a little more oil in the pan and pour in the egg and potato mixture. Sprinkle over the cheese and cook very gently for about 10-15 minutes, then either put under the grill or in the oven to finish cooking the top.

# The kitchen plate *continued*

# MAGICAL MUSHROOMS

*2 large cloves of garlic*
*50g chopped walnut pieces*
*50g pitted black olives*
*1 tin of anchovy fillets*
*5 tblsps olive oil*
*1 tblsp tomato purée*
*Juice of ½ a lemon*
*4 pinches of cayenne*
*400g tin of chopped tomatoes*
*1 tsp ground coriander*
*1 tsp ground cinnamon*
*475g of mushrooms, roughly*
*  chopped*
*1 small red pepper, finely chopped*
*Fresh coriander or parsley*

Put the garlic, walnuts, olives, anchovies, 4 tblsps olive oil, tomato purée, lemon juice, cayenne and tomatoes into a processor and whizz to make a smooth sauce. Put 1 tblsp olive oil in a large pan and add the ground coriander and cinnamon. Cook for 1 minute then add the sauce, cook for about 5 minutes and stir in the mushrooms. Cook for a further 5 minutes with the lid on. Take off the heat and leave to get cold. Just before serving add the finely chopped red pepper and herbs.

# TAPENADE

*350g jar of pitted olives*
*Drained tin of anchovies,*
*  roughly chopped – keep the oil*
*2 tsps capers, rinsed and drained*
*1 clove of garlic, roughly chopped*
*Olive oil*

Put the olives into a processor with the roughly chopped anchovies and their oil – I cut them up with scissors in the tin. Then add the capers and the garlic with about 2 tblsps of olive oil and whizz. Use more oil if necessary. Decant into a jar and place in the fridge where it will keep for at least a week.

# The kitchen plate *continued*

## HUMMUS

*200g tin of chickpeas, rinsed
    and drained*
*2 tsps lemon juice*
*2 cloves of garlic, crushed*
*1 tsp ground cumin*
*1 dstspoon tahini*
*Olive oil*

Put the above ingredients
into the processor and whizz.
You will need to add some
water to loosen it.
Sprinkle with paprika just
before serving.

## FRENCH BEANS

Cook some fine French beans
for a few minutes until just
al dente. Plunge into cold
water and drain well.
Dress with a little walnut oil
and some sea salt.

## PEPPERS

I buy peppers and slice them
into thin strips and cook
them in some olive oil very
gently in a covered pan with a
crushed clove of garlic for
about 20 minutes.
Add some balsamic vinegar to
the juices.

## BUTTER BEAN PUREE

*Tin of butter beans, rinsed
  and drained*
*Juice from ½ lemon*
*Clove of garlic, chopped*
*Small handful of mint leaves*
*Olive oil*
*Warm water*

Put the beans, lemon juice,
garlic, mint and some olive
oil into the processor and
give it a whizz. Add some
water to loosen it. Taste.

## TUNA AND WHITE BEANS

*1 tin of cannellini beans,
  drained*
*1 tin of tuna, drained and
  broken up*
*1 shallot or small onion, finely
  chopped*
*1 clove of garlic, crushed*
*Olive oil*
*Lemon juice*
*Parsley, finely chopped*

Mix all the above ingredients
together and taste.

WINE SUGGESTION
Yearlstone Number 3

# Main courses

# Genevieve's prawn curry

2 tblsps oil
1 onion, chopped
2 cloves of garlic, finely
 chopped
4cm fresh ginger, finely
 chopped
1 tblsp turmeric
1 tsp ground coriander
1 tsp ground cumin
1 tsp chilli powder
1 tsp mace
400g tin of chopped tomatoes
Juice and zest of a lemon
1 stick of cinnamon
450g raw prawns
Grating of nutmeg
Chopped fresh coriander
3-4 green chillies, finely
 sliced

I already know what you are thinking: that there are too many ingredients. I promise you that this recipe is very quick and absolutely delicious. You will make it time and time again.

Genevieve is my eldest daughter. She lives near Henley and has two children William, 10, and Gigi, 7. She is very artistic, paints beautifully, pots, makes lovely jewellery and is a brilliant cook when she wants to be. She has a real flair for it and just seems to throw it all together.

Put the oil in a pan and cook the onion gently until it softens. Add the garlic, ginger and the spices and cook for a minute or two. Add the tomatoes and then rinse out the tin with half the tin of water and stir it into the pan. Add the lemon zest and juice and the cinnamon stick. Simmer for 5 minutes uncovered and stir in the unshelled prawns. Continue to simmer for another 5 minutes until the prawns are cooked.
Just before serving stir in some nutmeg, the coriander and the chillies.

WINE SUGGESTION
Yearlstone Number 1

# Thai chicken (cold)

2 tsp green Thai curry paste
1 x 200ml carton of coconut
  cream
2 heaped tblsps lime
  marmalade
8 heaped tbsps mayonnaise
3 handfuls of chopped
  coriander
Juice and zest of a lime
8 cooked chicken breasts or the
  equivalent of cooked chicken

RICE SALAD
400g basmati rice
3 tblsps sesame oil
3 tblsps Nam Pla
  (Thai fish sauce)

This is a standard recipe for summer. So much nicer than Coronation Chicken which has been bastardised out of all recognition! Very easy to cook for a large group – I almost wish I wasn't giving away this recipe.

Mix together the curry paste, coconut cream, marmalade, mayonnaise, two handfuls of coriander and the zest and juice of the lime. Taste and add more curry paste if it needs it. Slice the chicken and add to the sauce. Serve with rice salad.

RICE SALAD: Cook the rice as usual and drain well. Add the sesame oil and fish sauce and mix well. Sprinkle the remaining chopped coriander and/or finely sliced spring onions through it to provide some colour.

WINE SUGGESTION
Yearlstone Number 1

# Middle Eastern shepherd's pie

750g potatoes, peeled
2 tblsps oil
2 tblsps pine nuts
2 medium onions, chopped
2 cloves of garlic, chopped
1 tsp ground cinnamon
Pinch of saffron, optional
2 tblsps chopped mint
2 tblsps chopped parsley
750g minced lamb
Juice of 1 lemon
400g tin of chickpeas, drained
   and rinsed
150ml stock
125g feta cheese, cubed
1-2 tblsps olive oil

This is fabulous. I like entertaining and this dish is ideal as it can all be done beforehand and just heated up. For eight people I tend to make two dishes so that I can put one at either end of the table and they can help themselves. It is essential to put tomato ketchup on the table – the relief on your guests' faces is one to watch for!

Cook the potatoes and mash them. Heat a large pan and add a little of the oil. Brown the pine nuts and remove them. Add some more oil and cook the onions and garlic until soft. Add the cinnamon and the saffron, if using, and half the mint and parsley. Stir in the lamb and cook until browned. Add the lemon juice. Mix in the chickpeas and the stock and simmer for 10 minutes until almost all the liquid has evaporated. Add the feta and the pine nuts with the rest of the mint and parsley. Season well. Cover with the potato. Drizzle with olive oil and cook at 200C/gas 6 for about 20 minutes.

WINE SUGGESTION
Yearlstone Number 3

# Moroccan potato stew with turmeric

*2 tblsps olive oil*
*85g onion, finely chopped*
*Thumb-sized piece of ginger,*
  *chopped very finely*
*500g red-skinned waxy potatoes,*
  *roughly chopped*
*½ tsp turmeric*
*½ tsp cumin*
*1 tsp paprika*
*Pinch of cayenne*
*2 tblsps freshly chopped coriander*

I don't really like vegetables with a few exceptions. Some of my friends say they could just eat vegetables but it is an after thought for me! However this and the recipe on the next page for aubergine stew are two that I can eat quite happily. Both are very popular in The Kitchen.

Put the oil in a medium-sized pan and sauté the onion until soft and translucent. Stir in the remaining ingredients. Pour in enough water to just cover. Mix well, bring to the boil, cover the pan and simmer very gently for 20 minutes. Crush one or two of the potatoes to thicken the sauce.

WINE SUGGESTION
Yearlstone Number 4

# Aubergine stew with halloumi, pine nuts and herbs

*This is very popular. I can even eat this and not miss meat too much.*
*A baked potato goes well if you need a bit more bulk.*

*4 tblsps olive oil*
*55g butter*
*300g red onions, chopped*
*3 cloves of garlic, chopped*
*400g tin of chopped tomatoes*
*1 tsp ground cumin*
*2 tsp castor sugar*
*300g aubergines, cut into*
  *bite-sized pieces*
*Good handful of walnuts or*
  *pine nuts*
*175g halloumi cheese*
*Handful of chopped mint*
*Handful of chopped coriander*

The only difference to this recipe when I make it in The Kitchen is to cook the aubergine in the oven if I happen to have it on for something else.

Heat 2 tblsps of the oil with the butter in a large frying pan; add the onions and cook over a gentle heat for 15 minutes. Add the garlic and cook for 2 minutes, then stir in the tomatoes, cumin and sugar. Take the pan off the heat. In a clean pan, heat all but ½ a tablespoonful of the rest of the oil and fry the aubergines until golden. Alternatively, mix the aubergine with the olive oil in a bowl, spread it over a baking tray and cook in the oven, preheated to 180c/gas 4, for about 30 minutes. This way you use less oil, as aubergines are very thirsty when they are fried.

Mix the tomato mixture and nuts with the cooked aubergine. Cut the halloumi into small chunks and fry in the remaining oil until golden. Add mint to the aubergine mixture and scatter the halloumi on top. Sprinkle with coriander and serve with a green salad.

WINE SUGGESTION
Yearlstone Number 3

# Pea and lentil salad

*200g Puy lentils*
*2 cloves of garlic*
*1 shallot, finely chopped*
*Juice of 1 lemon*
*4 tblsps olive oil*
*200g peas, frozen or fresh*

This is also a good vegetarian option – you could add some feta to this or even some prawns if you want to make it more of a main course. Mint is very refreshing in this especially in early summer when the herb seems to enhance nearly everything.

Cook the Puy lentils and garlic in unsalted water for 20 minutes until tender. Discard the garlic and drain the lentils. Add the shallot, lemon juice and oil while the lentils are still warm. Cook the peas and add to the lentils.

WINE SUGGESTION
Yearlstone Number 3

# Chicken tagine

3 tblsps olive oil
1 large onion, thinly sliced
2 cloves of garlic, crushed
4 chicken thighs, skinned
1 heaped tsp Ras el Hanout
1 tsp harissa paste
Zest and juice of ½ a lemon
Zest and juice of ½ a lime
2 tblsps runny honey
Chicken stock
Mint, freshly chopped

I don't really like fruit in my savoury meals but do add some apricots, prunes or nuts to this if you would like to. Ras el Hanout is the most wonderful Moroccan blend with all sorts of spices in it as well as rose petals! You will find it in your local supermarket as well as the harissa.

Heat half the oil in a heavy pan and fry the onions gently until soft, then increase the heat and brown them. Add the garlic and cook for a minute then remove the onions and the garlic from the pan. Add the rest of the oil to the pan and fry the chicken pieces until lightly browned.

Stir in the Ras el Hanout and harissa paste and cook for 1 minute. Add the lemon and lime juice and zest along with the honey, then pour some stock over the chicken – just enough to almost cover. Return the onions and garlic to the pan, mix well and add some of the chopped mint. Cover with a lid, and simmer over a very low heat for 20 minutes. Take off the lid, turn up the heat and reduce the juices until they become syrupy. Add the rest of the mint and serve with couscous (see page 44).

WINE SUGGESTION
Yearlstone Number 4

# Cous cous

200g cous cous
Stock powder
Lemon zest
Olive oil
Pistachio nuts, shelled
Pomegranate seeds
Fresh parsley

I find the best way of preparing cous cous is to put it in a bowl and add a small amount of stock powder, perhaps ½ tsp for four people. Pour on boiling water to cover with a thin layer – about 5mm. Stir and leave.

Then add whatever you like. I usually like to stir in a little lemon zest, a glug of good olive oil, some pistachio nuts and some pomegranate seeds, then sprinkle with some finely chopped parsley.

To get pomegranate seeds out of the fruit cut it in half and hold it, cut side down, over a dish. Bash the top hard with a wooden spoon.

WINE SUGGESTION
Yearlstone Number 3

# The Kitchen's good beef stew

*500g stewing beef, shin
  preferably*
*2 onions, roughly chopped*
*Olive oil*
*1 clove of garlic, roughly
  chopped*
*1 pack of pancetta or bacon
  lardons*
*Thyme*
*Red wine*
*Stock*
*Soy sauce*
*Butternut squash, carrots,
parsnips, turnips, etc*

I am sorry this is a bit of a vague recipe. A lot depends on what you have already in the way of vegetables. The bacon/pancetta makes a huge difference and the soy sauce is an essential. It adds a good depth of colour and flavour to the dish. A piece of orange rind is a good ingredient, but please don't feel that you have to add the ubiquitous tin of tomatoes. Somehow everything seems to taste the same – use them with discretion. Butternut squash, peeled and cubed is a very good addition.

When you are browning meat for a stew do it in small batches over a high heat and leave it alone. Every time you move it before it is dark brown it tears. Add it to the hot pan and then do something else for a minute or two before turning it. You need to get that brown caramelised colour for the flavour of the finished dish. If you add too much meat at a time it oozes juices and then it won't brown.

Fry the onions in the olive oil until browned and then remove. Add more olive oil to the pan and fry the meat in small batches and brown well. As they brown remove them and add them to the onions. With the last batch add the garlic and the thyme and after a couple of minutes pour in some wine and stock in equal quantities. Add the meat and onions to the sauce and simmer for 2 hours. Take off the heat and add the vegetables and cook for a further 30 minutes. Taste and add some soy sauce, about 1 tblsp and reduce the sauce if necessary.

WINE SUGGESTION
Yearlstone Number 4

# Spaghetti carbonara

225g fresh spaghetti or other
  thin pasta
75g pancetta
1 large egg
2 tblsps Parmesan, freshly
  grated
4 tblsps double cream
Parsley, freshly chopped

This is delicious and probably very fattening but "who cares..." I have had people come to me and say that they had no idea spaghetti carbonara could taste like this. I think they think it comes in a jar and is some sort of gluey, bechamel-type sauce. If you are not convinced please try this and let me know what you think.

The parsley makes a huge difference to the look of this dish.

Cook the pancetta until crisp and then drain on kitchen paper. Cook the pasta according to the directions. Whilst it is cooking put the Pancetta in a pan with the double cream and the Parmesan with a decent amount of black pepper. Warm through gently until the cheese melts in the cream. Just before serving take off the heat and add an egg. Mix well and then add the drained pasta to the pan with the sauce in it. Mix in well and serve sprinkled with parsley.

WINE SUGGESTION
Yearlstone Number 5

# Twice baked cheese soufflés

*50g butter*
*50g plain flour*
*300ml milk*
*Pinch of English mustard*
*Pinch of cayenne*
*110g strong cheddar cheese,
    grated*
*3 egg yolks*
*4 egg whites*
*200ml double cream*
*6 ramekins, buttered and
    floured*

These soufflés are so easy...if you can make a white sauce you can make these, I promise. They freeze very well so make them when life is calm and you have plenty of time. I make them in silicone muffin trays but you can make them in ramekins as well. Be sure to grease and flour them well. You will be so thrilled by them that you will make them regularly and start experimenting with flavours.

In a large saucepan, make a good white sauce with the butter, flour, milk and seasonings. Remove from the heat and stir in three quarters of the cheese and then the egg yolks. Whisk the egg whites until they form soft peaks and fold into the sauce. Spoon the mixture into the ramekins, place on a baking sheet and bake in the oven preheated to 190C/ gas 5 for 15 minutes. Remove the soufflés from the oven and allow them to cool and sink. Run a knife round the edges of the ramekins, turn out the soufflés and place them on an ovenproof dish.

Before serving, sprinkle the remaining cheese over the soufflés, season the cream and pour it all over the top, coating the soufflés completely. Turn up the oven to 200C/gas 6 and bake them for another 10 minutes until the tops are beginning to brown. Serve immediately.

WINE SUGGESTION
Yearlstone Number 5

# Desserts

# Lemon possett

400ml double cream
110g caster sugar
Juice of 2 lemons
Fresh raspberries

This is the easiest pudding in the world. It always amazes me that these simple ingredients put together form such a thick creamy pudding. It is very rich so serve in small glasses or coffee cups. I put it in those faux crumpled paper cups that are now so popular.

Bring the cream and the sugar to the boil and simmer for exactly 3 minutes, stirring occasionally. Take off the heat and whisk in the lemon juice. Strain through a sieve into 6 small glasses.

Leave for 4 hours before serving, garnished with fresh raspberries.

# Cappuccino mousse

*½ pint of very strong black*
  *coffee*
*1 packet of gelatine*
*4 tblsps sugar*
*300ml double cream*
*500ml ready-made custard*
*4 tblsps at least of Baileys or*
  *Tia Maria at least*
*1 tblsp cocoa powder*

This looks very good in small coffee cups, or small glasses – it really does look like a cappuccino especially if you can get the cream to the right floppy stage so that it folds over like foam.

Make the coffee and while it's still very hot, but not boiling, add the gelatine and the sugar and stir until both are dissolved. Allow to cool. Reserve 6 tblsps of the cream and whisk the rest until stiff. Stir in the custard and whisk well again. Add the liqueur and cooled coffee and whisk again. Pour into small cups or glasses and leave to set. Whisk the remaining cream and spoon over the top just before serving and sprinkle with a little cocoa.

# Chocolate roulade

*175g good quality 70% plain
  chocolate
5 eggs, separated
175g caster sugar
3 tblsps hot water
300ml double cream, whipped*

I have tried to introduce alternatives on the roulade theme but this is by far and away the favourite. I think sometimes the classics are best. This recipe also freezes well, you could try freezing it in individual slices as they don't take so long to thaw and go very well with a cup of tea in the afternoon. Raspberries, when in season, go very well with chocolate, either place them whole on top of the cream before you roll it up or as a sauce.

Line a Swiss roll tin with baking parchment. Break the chocolate into pieces and put in a bowl over hot but not boiling water, and allow to melt. Beat the egg whites until stiff. Beat the sugar and yolks together until light and pale in colour. Doing the beating in this order means you don't have to wash the beaters before tackling the egg whites. When the chocolate has melted add the hot water to the chocolate and mix gently. Add this to the egg yolks and mix lightly before folding in the egg whites.

Spread out into the tin and bake in an oven preheated to 180c/gas 4 for about 15 minutes. Remove the roulade from the oven and cover with a sheet of baking parchment, with a damp tea towel on top. Leave to get cold. Take off the cloth and the paper and spread the cake with the whipped cream. Fold over from the long side in. It will crack but this is inevitable so don't worry.

WINE SUGGESTION
Yearlstone Pink Fizz

Dust liberally with icing sugar and enjoy.

# Tunisian orange cake

200g caster sugar
150g ground almonds
1 level tsp baking powder
200ml sunflower oil
4 eggs
Zest of 1 large orange
Zest of 1 lemon

FOR THE SYRUP
Juice of orange
Juice of lemon
1 cinnamon stick
8 cloves
75g sugar

Okay – I have given in. So many people have asked for this recipe and I have always been very secretive about it but I am in a generous mood today.
This is by far and away the most popular pudding I make. It is a brilliant recipe.
Very easy to make and serve – it freezes well and is gluten free.

I have a customer who arrives at the kitchen gasping for a coffee and a piece of that cake. She leaves feeling much more at one with the world.

Line the 20cm round tin, 2" deep, with baking parchment or one of the natty liners available from the Lakeland shops. Mix the almonds with the sugar, baking powder and orange and lemon zest. Whisk the eggs with the oil and mix well into the dry ingredients. Bake in the oven preheated to oven 180C/350F gas mark 4 for 45-60 minutes until the cake is golden brown.

Make the citrus syrup by bringing the ingredients gently to the boil and simmering for 3 minutes. Leave to infuse. Leave the cake in the tin for 10 minutes then turn out.

I turn it upside down as it presents a better surface that way. Put on plate and pour over syrup. Place the cinnamon stick in the centre and the cloves around the edges.

WINE SUGGESTION
Yearlstone Vintage Brut

# Yearlstone vineyard

*"For wine that goes well with food"*

THE YEARLSTONE VINEYARD:
*an inside view of the Kitchen;*
*a bottle of the delicious rosé, Roger*
*and Juliet White - the owners of the*
*Vineyard; lunchtime on the Terrace*
*overlooking the Exe valley*

*The vineyard in autumn.*

# The dishes

SOUPS
Butternut Squash, Lime and Ginger
Pea and Mint Soup with Feta
Thai Vichysoisse
CHEESE
Twice Baked Cheese Soufflés
PASTA
Spaghetti Carbonara
FISH
Genevieve's Prawn Curry
Kedgeree
Smoked Fish Chowder
VEGETABLE DISHES
Aubergine Stew with Halloumi and Herbs
Moroccan Potato Stew with Turmeric
Cous cous
Pea and Lentil Salad
MEAT DISHES
Chicken Tagine
The Kitchen's Good Beef Stew
Middle Eastern Shepherd's Pie
Thai Chicken
PUDDINGS
Cappuccino Mousse
Chocolate Roulade
Lemon Possett
Tunisian Orange Cake
THE KITCHEN PLATE
Tortilla/Frittata
Magical Mushrooms
Tuna and White Beans
Hummus
French Beans
Butter Bean Purée
Tapenade
Peppers

# Acknowledgements

I want to say an enormous thank you to my friend, Clive Crook, for getting me to do this book. I really couldn't have done it without him. He has endlessly encouraged me to actually do what I have been talking about for years. His creativity and flair for design have made the book into something I feel really proud of.

Thank you also to Mark Davison for the photographs of the food.

Marcus Kinch for the photographs of Yearlstone. film41.co.uk

Thank you also to Roger and Juliet who own the Yearlstone Vineyard and who started up the café and provided endless advice and support especially in my first few weeks.

The decorative plates used for the cover, title pages and the Kitchen Plate are made by Halina Bayfield.

I also want to thank my customers and staff who have made my time at The Kitchen such fun - sometimes hectic and stressful - but they have been good humoured throughout and I have made many new friends.

Designer: Clive Crook
Sub Editor: Caroline Radula-Scott

Printed by: Ofset Yapimevi
Istanbul 00 90212 295 8601

Publishing consultant:
Roger Williams at Bristol Book Publishing
www.bristolbook.co.uk
ISBN: 978 0 9555376 5 3

# Notes